Garbage Collectors

Laura K. Murray

seedlings

CREATIVE EDUCATION • CREATIVE PAPERBACKS

Published by Creative Education and Creative Paperbacks
P.O. Box 227, Mankato, Minnesota 56002
Creative Education and Creative Paperbacks
are imprints of The Creative Company
www.thecreativecompany.us

Design by Ellen Huber
Production by Grant Gould
Art direction by Rita Marshall
Printed in the United States of America

Photographs by Alamy (Roger Coulam, Olga Ovchinnikova, Prostock-studio, Tetra Images LLC) Getty (Pramote Polyamate/Moment), iStock (Coprid, gautier075, kikira123, OpeartionShooting, PeopleImages, WendellandCarolyn), Shutterstock (aapsky, Florin Burlan, Chadolfski, I'm friday, MikeDotta, RMC42, Sirisak_baokaew, Xato)

Copyright © 2023 Creative Education, Creative Paperbacks
International copyright reserved in all countries.
No part of this book may be reproduced in any form
without written permission from the publisher.

ISBN 9781640264113 (library binding)
ISBN 9781628329445 (paperback)
ISBN 9781640005754 (eBook)

LCCN 2020907035

TABLE OF CONTENTS

Hello, Garbage Collectors! 4

Picking Up Trash 6

Many Places 9

Garbage Trucks 10

Hard Work 12

A Garbage Collector's Gear 14

What Do Garbage Collectors Do? 17

Thank You, Garbage Collectors! 19

Picture a Garbage Collector 20

Words to Know 22

Read More 23

Websites 23

Index 24

Hello, garbage collectors!

Garbage collectors pick up trash.

They take recycling, too.

Garbage collectors work in big cities and small towns. Often, two people work together.

One person drives the truck.

Some trucks have arms. The arms dump trash into the truck.

Garbage collectors lift heavy bags and bins. They work in the heat and cold.

They work in rain and snow.

They wear gloves and boots.

Some wear a mask. Bright clothes make them easy to see.

Garbage collectors sort trash. Most of it goes to a landfill. They keep cities clean.

Thank you, garbage collectors!

Words to Know

landfill: a place to get rid of trash

mask: a cover for the face

recycling: things like cans that can be used again

Read More

Kenan, Tessa. *Hooray for Garbage Collectors!* Minneapolis: Lerner Publications, 2018.

Leaf, Christina. *Garbage Collectors.* Minneapolis: Bellwether Media, 2019.

Websites

Garbage Truck Coloring Page
http://www.supercoloring.com/coloring-pages/garbage-truck

NASA Climate Kids: Recycle This!
https://climatekids.nasa.gov/menu/play

Note: Every effort has been made to ensure that the websites listed above are suitable for children, that they have educational value, and that they contain no inappropriate material. However, because of the nature of the Internet, it is impossible to guarantee that these sites will remain active indefinitely or that their contents will not be altered.

Index

arms 11
cities 9, 17
gear 14, 15
landfills 17
recycling 7
teamwork 9
trash 6, 11, 17
trucks 10, 11
weather 12, 13